Becoming His Dream Girl

A Bible Study for Young Ladies

Bernadine Zimmerman

Becoming His Dream Girl

A Bible Study for Young Ladies

Unless otherwise indicated, all Scripture quotations are taken from the Holy Bible, New Living Translation, copyright © 1996, 2004, 2007 by Tyndale House Foundation. Used by permission of Tyndale House Publishers, Inc., Carol Stream, Illinois 60188. All rights reserved.

Scripture quotations marked (MSG) are from THE MESSAGE, copyright © 1993, 1994, 1995, 1996, 2000, 2001, 2002 by Eugene H. Peterson. Used by permission of NavPress.

Scripture quotations marked ((NKJV) are taken from the New King James Version®. Copyright © 1982 by Thomas Nelson. Used by permission.

Scripture quotations marked (TLB) are taken from The Living Bible copyright © 1971. Used by permission of Tyndale House Publishers, Inc., Carol Stream, Illinois 60188.

THE HOLY BIBLE, NEW INTERNATIONAL VERSION®, NIV® Copyright © 1973, 1978, 1984, 2011 by Biblica, Inc.® Used by permission. All rights reserved worldwide.

Becoming His Dream Girl
A Bible Study for Young Ladies
Copyright © 2017 Bernadine Zimmerman

All rights reserved. This book or any portion thereof may not be reproduced or used in any manner whatsoever without the express written permission of the author except for the use of brief quotations in a book review.

Printed in the United States of America

All rights reserved.

Cover design: Alisa Hope Wagner
Cover model: Lashaunna Williams
Photographer: YU NGUYEN Photography

Dedication

This book is for

The tall girl and the short girl
The slim girl and the curvy girl
The confident girl and the insecure girl
The loud girl and the quiet girl
The bold girl and the shy girl
The girly girl and the tomboyish girl
The so-called good girl and bad girl
The girl who feels defined
and confined by labels
This is for you

Contents

Introduction

Section One…The Beginning of a Love Story

Chapter 1: A Forever Kind of Love
Chapter 2: The Perfect Gift

Section Two… Developing a Relationship

Chapter 3: Getting to Know Him
Chapter 4: Daily Bible Reading and Prayer

Section Three… All About You

Chapter 5: Your Reputation Precedes You
Chapter 6: Get Up and Get Moving
Chapter 7: Character Matters

Section Four…The Transformation

Chapter 8: Letting Go and Moving Forward
Final Thoughts

Acknowledgements
About the Author

Introduction

Dear Reader,

What do you dream about? I'm talking about the kind of dreaming where you write in your diary, talk with your friends, or just sit and daydream—fantasizing about the woman you want to become, the type of lifestyle you want to live... beautiful clothes, a big house, cool cars, a handsome guy...

Don't worry, I haven't been eavesdropping on your conversation or reading your journals. I was once a teenager, with a very active imagination. Over the years, I have dreamed about many different things. As with most people, some of my dreams came true, others changed as time went on, and some are still being worked on.

One of the most recurring dreams I had was meeting the perfect guy, planning the perfect wedding and having the perfect life... I don't know why I was thinking this way as a teenager, but when my best friends and I got together, part of the conversation was going to be about b-o-y-s.

For some reason, before young ladies even know what it means to truly love we are in love with the idea of love. We dream of finding the guy of our dreams, riding off into the sunset and living happily ever after. However, in our dreams do we ever evaluate ourselves to see if we are the girl he desires? What do we have to offer him, besides a pretty face and a sexy body? What makes us the girl of his dream?

Did I pique your interest?

Well keep reading and I'll tell you a secret that will help you in your quest to become the girl of his dreams. If I'm remembering my teenage years correctly, you probably already have a picture of a cute guy in your mind.

*Before you get too excited, the **"HIS"** I'm talking about, isn't the guy you're probably thinking about. Before you can become the girl of some guy's dreams, you need to become the girl of your Heavenly Father's dreams. Does that sound weird to you?*

Do you know that God has bigger dreams for you than you can ever have for yourself?

> *"'For I know the plans I have for you,' declares the LORD, 'plans to prosper you and not to harm you, plans to give you hope and a future.'"*
> *- Jeremiah 29:11 (NIV)*

*Your Creator has big plans for you. He wants you to have a great future. He has such high hopes for you that before you were even created He designed a plan for your life. He created you for a purpose. You were destined to be a young lady of excellence, integrity and impeccable character. He wants you to achieve your dreams. But first, He wants you to be the girl of **His** dreams. By now you're probably thinking, "God has a dream girl? I wonder, what's His type?" Well, join me on this quest and let's find out.*

But first, a little about me, your companion on this mission...

Who am I? I'm so happy you asked.

I'm Bernadine, a dreamer. I spent most of my childhood, teens and early adult years with my head in a book, lost in the make-believe world of fairytales and happily ever after.

I'm the girl who was caught by my math teacher in ninth grade with a romance novel hidden in my math book when I should have been trying to grasp the concepts found between the pages. Years later I cried through my college math course thinking it would end my dream of becoming a teacher because I had failed my midterm exam.

I'm also the girl who looked in the mirror and saw a pretty face on an ugly body and spent too many years feeling like I didn't measure up to society's idea of beautiful.

I write this letter to you my, dear reader because, although I am no longer a girl, I still hear the negative voices I heard as a young teen. They don't miraculously disappear when you become an adult.

For that exact reason, I have mentored and encouraged teen girls for most of my adult life. I started a small publication, "Keeping It Real Girl Talk," specifically for teen girls. I published it from 2000 -2010. I always wanted to inspire and encourage young women like you to be the very best that you can be despite your circumstances, your mistakes, and the roadblocks you encounter in life.

I have a desire to reach young women. In fact, this book that you're about to read began as a speech I gave to a teen girl group. I had a lovely time speaking to and interacting with them that night. I want to speak to you like I spoke to them.

I want to speak to the timid little girl in you; the one hidden behind the confident smile, well made-up face and stylish outfit. I want to tell her some of the things that you are going to find between the pages of this book.

If you've read this entire letter, I think we're now friends. So, keep reading my new friend, and let's see what it takes to be His dream girl.

Your friend,

Bernadine

Section One
The Beginning of a Love Story

Tanya closed the book with a dreamy sigh. She had been avidly devouring it for a few days. She'd lived through the ups and down that the hero and heroine went through in their relationship. Finally, in the last chapter he did what the heroine had been dreaming about all along. He told her that he loved her, got down on one knee and asked her to marry him.

"I can't wait to fall in love," Tanya thought falling back on the bed lost in her world of daydreams. I can't wait for the man of my dreams to sweep me into his arms and tell me he loves me forever and always...

Chapter 1
A Forever Kind of Love

> *"The great thing to remember is that though our feelings come and go God's love for us does not."* - C.S. Lewis

"I love you." Like in the story on the previous page, those three little words are featured prominently in many girls dreams. They dream of a knight in shining armor, or Prince Charming waltzing into their lives and sweeping them off their feet. The culmination of their dreams is when he whispers those three little words that make hearts flutter, faces flushed and palms sweaty.

"I love you."

And they lived happily ever after... fade out.

This is usually the perfect ending to a book or movie, and how many girls wish their dreams would end in real life. However, this is not how the story unfolds when we think about becoming the girl of our Heavenly Father's dreams. In His version of the love story, *I love you* is just the beginning.

Have you ever heard a song that made you long for love? (Shhh... Don't tell anyone, but I enjoy listening to love songs.) I've listened to countless love songs. When I listen to a song and the lyrics strike just the right emotional cord, the romantic, fairytale-believing, happily ever after girl in me swoons. Inside I'm thinking, "Can you imagine the guy you care about saying that to you? Your heart would probably be forever his."

Guess what, my dear friend? Someone already feels that way about you. Someone loved you with a forever kind of love, even before He met you, and His dreams brought you to life.

> *"Before I shaped you in the womb, I knew all about you. Before you saw the light of day, I had holy plans for you."*
> *- Jeremiah 1:5 (The MSG)*

Doesn't that make you feel special? This is proof that you are not a mistake. Before your mother ever met your father, God already knew all about you. He already had a destiny planned for you. He already loved you. Sometimes people get to know you, and then reject you. This rejection leaves you wondering, "What did I do wrong? Why did my best friend betray me? Why don't my friends want to be around me anymore? Is something wrong with me?"

With Jesus, you don't ever have to fear rejection. He loves you and wants you—faults and all. He knows every hidden thing about you and yet He loves you. There is no mistake that you have made or will ever make that God doesn't already know about. He still wants you! My dear young lady, you are more special to Him than you'll ever know. In this relationship, you won't have to forsake your values to feel loved. He offers His love freely. When He says, "I love you," He's not trying to get you into the back seat of a car or any other compromising position. Also, He won't tell you He loves you and then talk negatively about you to His friends. His love is the genuine article, the real deal, *a forever kind of love*.

I heard a preacher say once that all God ever wanted was you. He wants your love and your heart. The awesome thing is that He wants it with no strings attached and no hidden agendas.

On the television show, *The Bachelor*, the bachelor dates many ladies giving them a rose each week while trying to decide which girl he wants. Each week one lady doesn't receive a rose. Can you imagine being a contestant on that show, wondering week after week, "Is he going to give me a rose?" "Will I be his final choice?" Fortunately, you'll never have to wonder that about God. You were, are, and always will be His *first* choice. He wants to have a relationship with you. You are His treasured daughter. Within you is the ability to become everything He has called you to be. *Within you is the potential to become the girl of His dreams.*

Can I be God's Dream Girl?

You may wonder if it's possible to be the girl of someone's dream. You've been rejected many times. The memories of rejection may still sting. Most of us ladies have a memory of rejection. Try as you might, that feeling of being inadequate never quite leaves your mind or heart.

I'm no exception. I remember that sting and the lingering hurt. In my mind, I see the already insecure teenage girl that was me walking toward a shop. I was thinking about a new pair of sandals I had finally saved enough money to purchase. On my way, I passed two teenaged boys and I heard snippets of their conversation as I walked by.

One boy said, "She's pretty."

The other, "Yeah, but she's fat…"

She's fat, fat, fat, fat…

Why is it that negative words are the ones that lingered and played over and over in my mind like a stuck CD? Is it only me or do you also replay negative words?

We often allow negative words to define our lives. We allow them to shape our self-concept. We let words that people say thoughtlessly about us become huge barriers to our growth as individuals. We look at ourselves through their distorted lenses and become disenchanted with what we see. We begin to feel small and inferior to others around us. Those thoughtless, negative comments can have positions of power in our lives and strangle the positive things that others say. This should not be. We should NEVER let the opinions of others determine our self-worth.

Everyone has an opinion; however, just because someone sounds confident when expressing his or her opinion, does not make it a fact. Can I give you a word of advice? I know it's easier said than done but try to take it all in stride. There will always be people who talk about you as if they know you better than you know yourself.

If you model your life around some of the things people say about you, you'll never feel that you measure up! Their standards are impossibly high and you'd have failed before you even tried. **Know that you will always be enough for God**. With Him you'll always have dream girl status. How do I know this? There's a vast difference in being God's dream girl and being the girl of some guy's dreams.

If being God's dream girl was based on looks, many of us probably wouldn't fit the profile.

If it was based on athleticism some, would be left in the dust.

If being His dream girl was based on model behavior, most of us would certainly be disqualified.

Thankfully, being God's dream girl is not based on any of these things. God chose you just as you are in all of your imperfections. He sees potential on the inside of you. He chose you through the eyes of the heart.

Family, friends, or your number one crush may accept or reject you based on what you say, what you do, or how you look. Consequently, you're never quite sure of how to keep their love and acceptance. God looks beyond what He sees on the outside. He sees the inner you that those around you may not have taken the time to discover. They may pick out your personality traits and see them as negative.

Them - "She's so loud and outspoken."

God - "I can use that boldness to reach others."

Them - "She's so quiet."

God - "She has just the right thoughtfulness to listen to those who are hurting."

Them – "She doesn't dress like a nice girl should."

God - "I'm not interested in the clothes that she's wearing. I'm interested in her heart."

Them - "She has such a horrible past."

God - "She confessed and I've forgiven her."

Them – "She doesn't follow the rules of our church."

God – "She seeks after me, and *I* choose her."

Shouldn't it be the easiest thing to give your heart to someone who loves you, defends you, chooses you? Think about the worst day you've ever had. You threw a temper tantrum, hurt someone's feeling, disappointed your parents, or upset your best friend. At the end of that day, you couldn't think of one person you met that you didn't leave a negative impression on.

I've had those days as a teen and as an adult. I've sat down and looked at myself through an objective lens, cringed and thought, *"Did I do that? Did I say that?"* We all have those days where we say the wrong things and make the wrong choices. However, even after a day when you were at your very worst *God still loves you. He still chooses you.* He still wants you, your love, your heart. You are that precious to Him. He has placed such a high value on your heart that there is nothing you can do to make Him decide that it's not worth having anymore.

As you are coming to the close of this chapter my dear friend, (we're friends, right?) I want you to exhale. Release all the stress of other people's opinions.

They judge you by how you dress, what size you are, how you choose to do your hair and makeup, your personality and so many other things. However, they don't see the real you. There is a verse in the Bible that says, "People look at the outward appearance, but the Lord looks at the heart." - 1 Samuel 16:7 (NIV)

Hold that knowledge close to your heart and allow it to sink into your very being. Remind yourself of it on the days when you feel unwanted, unworthy or unloved. Tell yourself, *"God loves me more than I'll ever know. I'm His girl and He's always by my side."*

Dear Friend,

This chapter discusses a forever kind of love. If you're a happily ever after girl like me, the thought of beginning a relationship with someone who loves you with a forever kind of love should make you feel pretty special.

God's love for you is sweeter than the most beautiful love song you've ever listened to or the most inspirational, romantic love story you've ever read. *He loves you in spite of your perceived flaws and shortcomings. You never have to fear rejection with Him.*

Keep the thought of that forever kind of love in mind whenever the negative thoughts and hurts from the past try to get you down. God loves you forever and always. If He were giving out roses, He would always have one for you.

So as you continue this quest remember, you are His choice.

Your friend,

Bernadine

Time to Think!

If you're like me, thinking often starts with a little doodling, so...
doodle, add some color, get ready to think...

Shh... Secret Fact
about your quest companion

In college, my friend usually took my pen out of my hand because I doodled when I should have been listening.

Questions to Think About

1. List five qualities you think the guy of your dreams may be looking for in his dream girl.

2. Please rate each quality on a scale from 1 to 5 (1 being of low importance and 5 being of great importance). On a scale of 1-5 how do you think he would rate you?

3. Did you measure up? How did you feel if you didn't get a perfect 5?

4. Based on what you've read in this chapter, what do you think is the difference between how God sees you and how a potential date may see you?

5. What is something that you don't ever have to fear with Jesus?

6. What is it that God desires to have with you?

7. *Memories of rejection linger for a long time.* Do you remember a time when you experienced rejection? If you were able to move on, how did you get past it?

8. Write out Jeremiah 1:5. Replace "you" with your name.

9. Read the above verse with your name again. How does it make you feel to know that God thinks this way about you?

10. What is one personality trait you have that people may view negatively but can be used to do something positive for God?

Chapter 2
The Perfect Gift

"Give your heart to God, and He will look after it." - anon

So now back to the beginning of the "I love you." In a normal relationship, you get to know someone and then decide whether you can trust him with your heart. God does it a little differently. You could say He does it in reverse. The first thing He requires you to do when you enter a relationship with Him is *give Him your heart*.

God makes it easy for you to give Him this extraordinary gift. He doesn't just say to you, "I love you." He shows you in such a way you cannot doubt His love for you. He makes sure that you know that **you** are His choice.

> *"For God so loved the world that he gave his one and only Son, that whoever believes in him shall not perish but have eternal life."*
> *- John 3:16 (NIV)*

Romans 5:7-9 further states:

> *"Very rarely will anyone die for a righteous man, though for a good man someone might possibly dare to die. But God demonstrates his own love for us in this: While we were still sinners, Christ died for us." (NIV)*

Take a moment and think on those verses. Let it sink in. *God loves you!* Isn't it mind boggling just how much the Creator of the Universe loves you, loves me, loves all of us? You don't have to be afraid to tell Him, "I love you." When He sent His Son to die on an old rugged cross, He told you first.

He says it to you every day in every possible way. Every breath you take is a testament of God's love for you. I can't find enough words to express the sense of wonder and awe that I feel when I sit and reflect on just how much He loves me.

Before God ever asked you for your heart, He demonstrated how much He loved you by giving His Son to die for you. However, He doesn't ask you to prove anything to Him. Your boyfriend may ask you to prove your love but still doesn't stick around. All God asks of you in that first instant is to *give Him your heart*.

The concept of giving your heart first may seem a little strange. The logical thing would be to give your heart only after you really get to know someone, but God's ways are beyond our understanding. Proverbs 23:26 states*: "O my son **(daughter),** give me your heart. May your eyes take delight in following my ways."*

I still remember the day I gave my heart to Him. It was the best decision I ever made. I grew up in an environment where, thanks to my parents, I went to church whether I wanted to or not. I knew about Jesus, but I didn't decide to follow Him until I was a teenager. I thought I was a good person and that should be enough, but it wasn't. On the day that I came to that realization that being good wasn't enough, my life changed. Here's a little of my story:

My Testimony:
Beginning a New Life in a High School Library

It was the unlikeliest of places for it to happen. The most likely place would have been in one of the weekly church services my parents made me attend.

Maybe it had to do with my love of books. Whatever the reason, there I was, tears streaming down my face in my high school library.

It was my eleventh-grade year and the Christian Student Movement Club was having a week of activities. I wasn't a part of the club, but I had accepted a friend's invitation to attend one of their events. They were showing a movie called "Thief in the Night."

I cried through the entire movie because I saw myself reflected in the main character, a woman who was knowledgeable about God but did not have a relationship with Him. In the end, she realized that knowledge without relationship wasn't enough.

By the time the credits started rolling and the song, "I Wish We'd All Been Ready," started playing in the background, I knew it was time to decide. When the club's chaplain asked if anyone wanted to give their life to Christ, I was ready. I did it.

In my high school library, I said yes to Jesus, and there began my new life in Christ.

It has been over 20 years since I made the decision to give my heart to Christ. I have never regretted it. I remember one of my proudest moments after I accepted Christ as a teenager was when my mother told me a few weeks later, *"Baby, I know you got saved. I can see a change in you."* She told me there was a change from my sometimes-surly attitude—especially when I was called upon to do chores, like washing dishes.

Don't get me wrong, I didn't suddenly become the perfect teenager. I still made mistakes, but I knew that in Christ I'd always find forgiveness. Today, Christ is still number one in my life. I am never alone because He is always with me. He guides my decisions and because of Him I make less mistakes than I would trying to navigate life on my own (if I'd only listen to Him more, I'd make even less mistakes).

If you sit down and over think it or have a heart to heart talk with your girlfriends who have not made a choice to give Christ their heart, it can seem complicated. You will probably come away from the conversation with a list of things you think you'll never be able to do again.

You are likely to leave focusing on what they say you're going to lose out on by choosing Christ. The emphasis becomes a list of the perceived "cans" and "cannots" of Christianity. The perceived losses instead of real gains. When I made the choice to give my heart to Christ, I didn't think of any of these things. He never asked me to. He wanted me in whatever state I was in. He wanted my love and my heart. God's standards never change. *He always starts with the heart.*

Don't overthink it.

Don't over complicate it.

Giving Him your heart is as simple as it sounds. It's a personal decision that only you can make. It means asking Him to forgive you for your sins, and allowing Him to come into your heart.

> *"If you confess with your mouth that Jesus is Lord and believe in your heart that God raised him from the dead, you will be saved. For it is by believing in your heart that you are made right with God, and it is by confessing with your mouth that you are saved."*
> *- Romans 10:9-10 (NLT)*

That's not difficult at all, is it? Giving your heart to God is the best gift you can give Him. Have you ever searched and searched for a special gift for someone that you loved? You spent more money than you could afford on it. However, they didn't act as if they appreciated your gift. They treated it as if it was something of little or no value.

When you accept Christ into your heart, He doesn't treat your gift as if it has no value. He treasures the gift of you. He sees it as priceless. He brags about it. Heaven throws a party to commemorate the event. Think about that, dear girl. *Heaven celebrates you!* In the book of Luke Jesus tells the parable of a woman who has ten coins and loses one. She searches until she finds it. When she finds, it she is so excited that she throws a party.

The Parable of the Lost Coin

> *"Or suppose a woman has ten silver coins and loses one. Doesn't she light a lamp, sweep the house and search carefully until she finds it? And when she finds it, she calls her friends and neighbors together and says, 'Rejoice with me; I have found my lost coin.' In the same way,*

*I tell you, there is rejoicing in the presence of
the angels of God over one sinner who repents."*
- Luke 15:8-10 (NIV)

Let your heart reflect on that... the angels in heaven *pause*, *rejoice* and *throw a praise party* to celebrate your decision. If you haven't already asked Jesus into your heart, take a moment and do so. When you do that, *you become His*. You belong to Him.

Dear Friend,

*If you truly want to be **His** dream girl but haven't yet given Him your heart, why don't you do that before going any further? Simply take a moment and pray this prayer with me.*

Dear God, I realize that I am a sinner. Please forgive me for my sins, come into my heart and help me to become the girl of Your dreams. Help me be the girl You created me to be. In Jesus' name, Amen!

If you prayed that prayer and truly meant it, you are a child of God. If you have prayed, send me an email. I want to rejoice with the angels as they rejoice for you.

"I tell you, there is rejoicing in the presence of the angels of God over one sinner who repents.*" - Luke 15:8-10 (NIV)*

Welcome to the family dear friend… you are on your way to becoming His dream girl.

In Christ's love,

Bernadine

Time to Think!

What's going through your head right now? **Doodle, add some color, get ready to think...**

Shh... Secret Fact
about your quest companion

I love writing and receiving letters. You can probably tell from the letters I've written in this study.

Questions to Think About

1. What is the first thing God requires from you when you begin a relationship with Him?

2. What is the main difference in the way you begin a relationship with God and the way you begin a normal relationship?

3. How did God demonstrate His love for you?

4. In your own words, what does it mean to give God your heart?

5. What happens in heaven when you give your heart to God?

6. What do you think you lose by giving your heart to God? Explain.

7. What do you gain by giving your heart to God? Explain.

8. Have you already given your heart to God? If the answer is yes, share how it happened below.

9. If you were asked to memorize a Bible verse quoted in this chapter, which verse would it be and why?

10. Finish the following note to God:

Dear God,

I've never thought about becoming Your dream girl. However, now that I have, I find the idea…

Section Two
Developing a Relationship

It was a whirlwind courtship. Alaina and Tom had fallen madly in love. Despite their parents' protests they decided to get married. After all they were eighteen and nineteen, and old enough to know when they were truly in love. They had met at a Youth Meeting at his church when she was visiting with friends. They caught each other's attention right away and spent the entire meeting sneaking glances at each other.

Three months later they were sure they were destined to be together forever. He loved her beautiful eyes so he spent most of his time gazing into them while pretending to listen to what she was saying. She was impressed by his bulging biceps so she never explored further to see the type of person he was on the inside.

Chapter 3
Getting to know Him

"Most of us know about God, but that is quite different from knowing God." - Billy Graham

At the beginning of this chapter is a story about a young couple, Alaina and Tom who are planning on getting married. Do you think their marriage will last? I admit I have a few doubts, the first being the fact that the two made no real effort to bypass the physical attraction and get to know each other. Before you romantic, "happily ever after" types get upset with me, I do have a confession to make. I'm a bit of a romantic, too.

I've heard and read a story or two (or hundreds) about love at first sight. I've even had my own fanciful daydreams about knowing he, the man of my dreams, was *the one* the moment I saw him.

So, is it true? Is love at first sight real? I haven't proved or disproved it yet so we'll assume that maybe, just maybe, it is possible. Maybe you can fall in love with someone without really knowing them. However, after a while the excitement and romantic glow fades. It's just the two of you. You may find yourself wishing you had taken a little more time to get to know each other. I think it's a tragedy to give your heart so quickly and find out that you really don't like and respect the person you gave it to.

This won't happen with God. The more you learn about God, the more you fall in love with Him. Then just when you think you couldn't possibly love Him anymore, you learn something about Him that causes you to fall even more deeply in love with Him.

When you first fall in love with God, you are putting your most valuable possession in the hands of someone you don't really know. You take a leap of faith although you're not sure that person you've given your heart to can live up to your expectations.

As you continuously read His word, you find yourself becoming really fascinated and in awe at the depths of His love for you. His words at times seem like a personal love letter that draws you in and causes tears to fall from your eyes. Which girl doesn't love a love letter that comes from the heart written just for her?

As you get to know God, you'll experience His love in a whole new way. You'll find out that His love for you is deeper than you ever imagined. His love is unwavering, without measure and without ending. Here's a few things I've come to realize about God's love:

- *God's love for us goes beyond the sappiness of the fairy tale.*

- *His love transcends the dreams of happily ever after.*

- *His love is like a mother's loving hug assuring you that everything will be alright on the days when it seems like everything is going wrong.*

- *God's love is like comforting, reaffirming words whispered in your ear after a horrible day when not one person had something positive to say to you.*

- *His love is like the promise of a better tomorrow after you were bruised, broken and sad over everything that went terribly wrong today.*

- *God's love is all of that and more than words can explain. God delights in you. He loves you. He knows you inside out and He wants you to know Him the same way.*

I remember when my siblings and I would visit my mom in the hospital. She couldn't speak, but we could always tell she was happy to see us. However, there were times her eyes would search the room until they connected with the eyes of my dad. Her facial expression would relax and soften. Her eyes would get brighter with a little smile appearing on her face. She was in the presence of the one she had loved for most of her life. Someone she knew inside out and who knew her the same way. After over forty years of marriage they knew each other intimately. They had spent so much time in each other's presence that they sometimes seemed able to communicate without words.

God knows you even more intimately. Before you were formed in the womb, before the foundation of the earth God knew you. He knew the plans He had for you and He knew the choices you would make.

God loves you even though He knew the times you would reject His predestined plan for your life and choose another way. He knows your deepest, darkest secret, but it is not terrible enough that He will ever turn His back on you. He wants you to get to know Him as well.

You've given the most valuable thing you possess to Him. When you tell someone that you've given your heart to Jesus, you should be able to tell them all about this Jesus. Who is He? What makes Him special enough to give your heart to Him? So, your next question will probably be: *"How do I get to know God?* It's not like we can sit across from each other and have a chat over pizza."

I assure you, it's quite simple. We get to know God by:

1. Going to church and spending time with other believers.
2. Reading, studying and memorizing His word.
3. Spending time in prayer, simply talking with Him.

Do I have to Go to Church?

One of my favorite verses of Psalm is the one where David said, *"I was glad when they said unto me, let us go into the house of the Lord."* Whenever I read it, I imagine it being said in the exuberant voice of my childhood pastor.

Psalm 122 and verse 1 says, "I was glad when they said unto me, come let us go into the house of the Lord..."

Somehow, my pastor made it seem like church was the place to be. It sounded as exciting as any popular young people's hotspot.

During my childhood, teen and young adult years, there was a concerted effort in my community to involve us in church. We had Sunday School, youth meetings, Bible trivia, memory verse contests, drama productions and other fun events to keep our attention as young people. We were encouraged by our youth leaders and others within the church to give Jesus our hearts, get to know Him and live a life that would honor Him.

We showed up weekly with anticipation of having fun together as youths. However along the way for many of us lifelong changes took place. We formed relationships and began to develop our personal value system as we gained knowledge about the word of God. For me, being involved in church was an invaluable part of my early Christian walk and it still is.

What about you? *Do you go to church often?* As a new Believer one of the first pieces of advice you're given is usually to be sure to attend church. It really is an important part of being a Christian. God wants us to get together with other Believers to worship Him. There are numerous benefits to being a part of a church body:

- *You feel a part of a community and less alone.*

- *You gain strength and wisdom from others who are on the same journey as you.*

- *You have others to encourage, counsel and help you to understand God's Word.*

- *You gain a deeper understanding of Scripture as a new Believer when you're able to study and discuss with others.*

- *Your faith in God, your Creator, becomes stronger and more real as you hear His Word being preached on a regular basis.*

- *You become more confident in who you are as a Christian as you observe the lives of godly men, women and even your peers who have made the decision to give their hearts to Christ.*

Getting to know God doesn't stop with attending church. If you only read your Bible, pray and think about God when you are in church, you will never truly know Him. Your relationship will be like that of acquaintances where you exchange meaningless chitchat occasionally, but there is no real depth to the relationship.

Believing that you know God because you go to church is like saying that you know your favorite singers because you heard a few talk show hosts talk about them.

I can imagine the conversation:

You – "You wouldn't believe what my friend (Insert your favorite singer's name) said the other day…"

Friend –Wow! "You know (_____)?"

You – "Of course! She's a good friend of mine."

Friend – "When did you meet her? Can you introduce me? I want to meet her."

You – "Well… I haven't really met her…"

Friend – "I'm confused, I thought you said she's your friend."

You – "Well I kinda, sorta heard a few talk show hosts talking about her…"

… awkward silence…

Seems silly, right? You'd never call a person your friend if you don't know them personally. You truly get to know someone when you spend time in their presence, actively engaging them and finding out information about them. What are their likes and their dislikes? What makes them happy or sad? What do they enjoy doing? So, you probably want to know how this applies to developing a relationship with God. Well, *we will continue our quest on how to get to know God in the next chapter.*

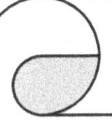

Dear Friend,

I hope that you have been finding this quest to be an informative one. My prayer is that it causes you to think about God in a more personal way.

In this chapter you've begun to learn about the importance of getting to know God and developing your relationship with Him. Going to church is a huge part of learning more about God.

If you don't attend church regularly, I hope that you'll consider finding a church home. There are so many benefits to being a part of a church where you'll hear the Word of God and be encouraged to grow into the person that He wants you to become.

*Remember, "**So faith comes from hearing, that is, hearing the Good News about Christ."** - Romans 10:17 (NLT)*

God's girl,

Bernadine

Time to Think!

*Time for a little doodling break... so doodle **an Emoji of your thinking face,** add a border, some color, get ready to think...*

Shh... Secret Fact
about your quest companion

> I started writing letters to God when I was a teenager. It's something I still do regularly.

Questions to Think About

1. Do you think love at first sight is real? Explain.

2. What can happen when people rush into relationships?

3. How do you get to know God?

4. What happens when you begin to get to know God more intimately?

5. List three things you've discovered about God's love.

6. List three benefits of going to church.

7. Do you go to church regularly? If the answer is yes, share the impact attending church has had on your life.

8. Do you think it's possible to truly get to know God by simply attending church? Explain.

9. How do you truly get to know someone?

10. If you were asked to memorize a Bible verse quoted in this chapter, which verse would it be and why?

Chapter 4
Daily Bible Reading and Prayer

"If you don't have time to pray and read your scriptures, you are busier than God ever intended you to be." —Anonymous

Do you know that if you're a Christian you are supposed to feed yourself spiritually just as you feed yourself physically? If you're a new Christian you're wondering, *"spiritual food? What's that?"* 1 Peter 2:2 states

> *"Like newborn babies, crave pure spiritual milk, so that by it you may grow up in your salvation." (NIV)*

When you accept Christ, spiritually you are like a newborn baby. The word of God is your spiritual food. In order to grow spiritually you must spend time reading the Bible and talking to Him while He talks to you. As a consequence of doing this, you will begin to deepen your relationship with Jesus Christ and become a stronger Christian. *"That sounds like too much time and effort,"* you may be thinking. However, think about the relationships you've formed over your lifetime. I'm sure you'll agree that every relationship takes work to develop into something with depth that will survive during different seasons in your life.

I met my friend, Mandie, almost twenty years ago in an online Christian Women's chat room. When we met, we knew nothing about each other except that she was a third-year teacher from South Carolina, and I was a second-year teacher from the Bahamas and we were both Christians.

Over the years of our friendship, we've exchanged thousands of emails, phone calls, text messages and snail mail. I've visited her and her family in South Carolina and she's visited me in the Bahamas.

We met in person for the first time when I visited after four years of friendship. We were about to leave a restaurant when it started to rain. I was quite content to sit and wait for the rain to stop because my hair + the rain = oh no! However, without being asked, she ran through the rain to get an umbrella because I refused to get my hair wet.

When I visited a few years later, she traveled with an umbrella everywhere we went, **just in case it rained**. *While she had no problem getting wet in the rain, she remembered that I did.*

We've shared many milestones in our lives although we live far apart. We've comforted each other through deaths of loved ones and celebrated births, weddings and other milestones in each other's lives.

The southern belle and the small-town island girl somehow developed a "real life" relationship based on friendship and trust although we lived in different countries. We didn't know in the beginning that we'd become bonded like family. We simply put in the effort. The result was a beautiful sisterhood and friendship that I'm glad I didn't miss out on.

Just as you would spend time in your friends' presence getting to know them, so you truly get to know God when you spend time reading the Bible and talking to Him. As you get to know Jesus Christ more personally, you will find that you're not comfortable doing certain things you did before. There may be attitudes and behavior that you displayed before that change. You're putting away the old things you used to do that were not in keeping with the standards God expects of His children. This is an example of you growing spiritually into a mature Christian.

So dear girl, desire spiritual food and feed yourself often. This is the one food you can eat as much as you want and not gain one unwanted pound. Sounds too good to be true, right? Why don't you try it and see? Don't ever stop reading. I promise the only thing you'll develop is spiritual muscles and a beautiful, strong relationship with God because you put in the effort required to get to know Him.

When you spend time with God, you'll find that He is so much more than what the preacher says, what your Sunday school teacher says or even what your parents say. You'll find out that God is the Friend that surpasses all other friends.

- He doesn't have mood swings or bad days where He decides He doesn't want to talk to you, so He's going to let the phone go to voicemail.

- He doesn't tell you that He really isn't interested in hearing your problems and could you please talk about something else.

He doesn't do these things because everything about you concerns Him, and He wants to be the One who you share everything that is on your heart with.

If God is so concerned with everything about you, shouldn't you feel the same way about getting to know Him? **Spend**

time in His Word. It may seem difficult at first, but if you'll try to read the Bible and get to know God, you'll never regret it.

When I became a Christian, there were times when the focus seemed to be more on a list of do's and don'ts of Christianity than on a real relationship with God. I often found it to be very restrictive. I asked lots of questions and often the answers I was given didn't satisfy me.

I determined that I was going to forge my own path, talk to God for myself and see what His Word said. I had given my heart to Him and I needed to know that He was worthy of it. I wasn't just going to take my parents' or my pastor's word for it. I wanted to form my own opinion.

I committed to reading the Bible on a regular basis. At first, I found it boring and virtually impossible to understand. I didn't give up though. I had my insatiable love of reading going for me. I devoured mysteries, romance, suspense, biographies almost any book I could get my hands on, *except* the Bible. I decided I would try to fall in love with what I considered a boring old book. So, I began to look for romance, mystery and intrigue between the pages and guess what? *I found it!*

I fell in love with the men and women of the Bible, and I spent many hours during my teen years just reading their life stories. I began to learn more about my Heavenly Father as I read. There are many things that stood out to me as I tried to get to know my Heavenly Father.

He loves me more than I can ever imagine.

He will never forget about me or forsake me.

I matter to Him.

Over the years, I've read many Scriptures about God's love. I can quote many of them. However, one Scripture became real to me at a time in my life when I needed it most. Shortly after my mother died, I was reading the following verses:

> *"Can a mother forget her nursing child? Can she feel no love for the child she has borne? But even if that were possible, I would not forget you! See, I have written your name on the palms of my hands." - Isaiah 49:15-16 (NLT)*

I had read those verses many times. This time it felt as if it was written just for me. The words blurred on the page as the tears began to flow down my face. Memories of my mom flooded my mind. The memory that I'm about to share with you stood out.

It was after a particularly difficult day at work that I went home depressed and upset about a situation I was dealing with. When I opened the door, my mother, who was visiting, was sitting on the couch facing the door. I took one look at her and started crying in the doorway. I didn't have to be strong anymore.

She opened her arms wide and simply said, "Come here, Baby." I quickly ran into those opened arms that had always protected me. She pulled my head to her chest and gently stroked my hair while I cried as if my heart was broken. "Don't cry, Baby. Everything will be all right" was all I heard until my tears were well spent. Then, she started praying for me that God would give me peace about every situation in my life that was proving too difficult for me to handle.

That bittersweet memory of my mother holding me while I cried made the verse in Isaiah come alive to me. In the safety of my mother's arms, I knew without doubt that I was loved unconditionally. As I read that Scripture, I realized that although my mother's arms would never be there to hold me close again, God's arms would always be there.

- He loves me more than my mom who loved me, held me, defended me and believed in me; more than anyone else on this earth.
- He loves me so much that He has my name engraved in the palm of His hand.
- He loves me so much that He always has time for me.
- He never gets tired of me wanting to be in His presence.
- He wants my time and attention.

The time I spent reading the Bible and talking to God as a teenager solidified the foundation of my walk with God. It allowed me to get a glimpse of just who God is and caused my initial schoolgirl love of the heroic God who died for me to begin to develop into something stronger and something lasting that would endure beyond my school days and for the rest of my life.

Reading the Bible will do that for you also. The time you spend reading, studying, and memorizing God's Word causes Him to become real to you. You begin to think of Him as a friend and confidant. You want to do things to please Him and do nothing that would hurt Him. Without even realizing it, you find yourself praying. Sometimes it may feel like prayer is something difficult to do. It's not; it's simply talking to the Person you've given your heart to.

How do I Pray?

"My heart has heard you say, 'Come and talk

with me.' And my heart responds, 'Lord, I am coming.'" - Psalm 27:8 (NLT)

Prayer is simply sharing with God what's on your heart. It involves opening your heart to God and letting Him know how much you love and trust Him. God loves those moments when His children choose to simply spend time in His presence, talking to Him.

God wants you to talk to Him about everything. Whatever is important to you, you can talk to God about it. There is nothing that concerns you that He will find unimportant.

- *The hurtful words someone said that wounded you concerns Him.*

- *The daily decisions you make concerns Him.*

- *Your thoughts about the future concerns Him.*

- *Everything about you is important to Him.*

Prayer is something you can do throughout the day without even thinking. The more you do it, the more natural it becomes until it is almost as natural as breathing. You can talk to God about every aspect of your life. Even the seemingly mundane details of your life don't have to escape your conversation with Him.

I don't know if He gets bored with some of the things I talk to Him about, like *"God please give me an idea of what to wear tomorrow or how to make this outfit look a little different."* (Yes, I use God as a fashion consultant). Sometimes it's, *"God I'm not sure why I'm feeling this way about this person, but I need You to help me to get over my anger."* Or sometimes it's, *"God search my heart, and show me those areas you want me to change."* The list goes on and on.

I feel free to talk to God about the minor and major details in my life because it was modeled before me when I was growing up. My mom was a firm believer in prayer. She made talking to God seem a normal part of life. There were times she knelt to pray. However, most times, I simply observed her praying as she went about her daily routine. Whether she was cooking or cleaning, she made prayer a part of it. She prayed about everything. So, *I knew that I could talk to God anytime, anywhere and about anything.* Guess what? You can make prayer an integral part of your life too.

What Should I Pray About?

Pray about the things you are thankful for… "Always giving thanks to God the Father for everything, in the name of our Lord Jesus Christ." - Ephesians 5:20 (NIV)

Pray about the things you need to be forgiven for… "If we confess our sins, He is faithful and just to forgive us *our* sins and to cleanse us from all unrighteousness." - 1 John 1:9 (NKJV)

Pray about the things that make you not want to forgive… "And be kind to one another, tenderhearted, forgiving one another, even as God in Christ forgave you." - Ephesians 4:32 (NKJV)

***Pray about the things that worry you*: school, friends, peer pressure, the future…** "Don't worry about anything; instead, pray about everything." - Philippians 4:6 (TLB)

Pray about the things that make you afraid… "Whenever I am afraid, I will trust in You." - Psalm 56:3 (NKJV)

Pray about God's will for your life… "For I know the plans I have for you," declares the LORD, "plans to prosper you and not to harm you, plans to give you hope and a future." - Jeremiah 29:11(NIV)

Pray about everything! Nothing that concerns you is too small for God to be bothered with or too big for Him to handle. You are His top priority.

Listen for His Voice

Have you ever been in a conversation where the other person talked, talked, talked and you just listened? You waited patiently until they were finished hoping to be able to express your thoughts, but when they were finished so was the conversation. Unfortunately, we can get into the habit of treating God this way. We tell Him everything that is on our hearts and before He can respond the conversation is over.

If you find yourself doing that, remember in a real relationship the conversation is never one sided. If we want to develop a great relationship with God, you should always be ready to listen to Him. As you spend time in His presence, it will become easier to identify His voice.

You'll recognize His voice in the thought that whispers, "*No!*" when you're about to do something you know you shouldn't do.

You'll recognize His voice when you read Scripture or hear a sermon that speaks to exactly what you're dealing with.

You'll recognize it in words of wisdom from trusted family and friends. Just as a mother or father's voice becomes so familiar to a baby that they can recognize it above every other voice, so will His voice become familiar to you.

A conversation is sweeter when both parties participate. After all, isn't that what relationship is all about? *As you get to know Him and who He is, you will begin to take on His character traits. You cannot truly know Him and not want to be more like Him.*

Dear Friend,

As you can see, I thought prayer and Bible reading were such an important part in developing your relationship with God that they got a whole chapter. Above all things, I hope this chapter showed you why prayer and Bible study should be a daily habit in your quest to get to know God.

You'll never get the full benefit of giving your heart to God if you don't take the time to learn His heart.

He knows you inside and out. From numbering the hairs on your head to capturing your tears in a bottle, God delights in everything about you.

Spend time with other Believers, read His Word, talk to Him... get to know Him. *To know Him is to fall in love with Him all over again. I know as I study His Word and gain new knowledge from the Bible, I just love Him even more.*

His lifelong learner,

Bernadine

Time to Think!

*More questions ahead, time for a little doodling break... so doodle **an emoji reading a bible or praying,** add a border, some color, get ready to think...*

Shh... Secret Fact
about your quest companion

I loved when my students decorated their test papers with a pretty border before I displayed it on the bulletin board.

Questions to Think About

1. What is spiritual food?

2. What must you do in order to grow spiritually?

3. Describe the last time you made a new friend. How can you use the same strategy you used to get to know your friend to develop a relationship with God?

4. What is prayer?

5. Do you feel closer to God when you pray? Explain.

6. Why is it important to spend time reading the Bible?

7. In this chapter, the author wrote that the verse, Isaiah 49:15-16, illustrating God's love, became real to her after her mother died. *Describe a time you experienced God's love in a real way.*

8. How can reading your Bible and praying change your perception of God?

9. If you were asked to memorize a Bible verse quoted in this chapter, which verse would it be and why?

10. Finish the following note to God:

Dear God,

I want to get to know You intimately. Here's what I plan to do…

Section Three
All About You

Sandra's Regret

Sandra pulled her jacket tighter to her chest as she tried to ignore the stares and whispers that followed her down the hall. It had been that way since she came back to school. She had once been the most popular girl in school. She had been the head of the cheerleading team, president of the debate team and a straight A student, but that was last year. This year she was popular for all the wrong reasons.

"It's amazing how things can change so quickly," Sandra thought to herself as she walked into the restroom, which thankfully was empty. "One date changed my entire life!"

"I can't believe it's been three months!" she mused. "People are treating me as if I'm some freak show. I know I made a mistake. I shouldn't have gotten into the car with someone who had been drinking, but I'm still the same person I was last year."

Sandra stared at her reflection in the mirror. Tears began to pool in her eyes. The right side of her face, once unblemished, was covered with tiny scars from the broken glass that had cut her. "No wonder they think I'm a monster," she thought, as she looked away and limped out of the restroom. She wished she could be invisible, so she didn't have to face the stares and whispers again.

Chapter 5
Your Reputation Precedes You

> *"A reputation once broken may possibly be repaired, but the world will always keep their eyes on the spot where the crack was." - Joseph Hall*

The story on the previous page is an excerpt from a short story that originally appeared in *Girl Talk Magazine*. I thought it was a good introduction to this chapter. It's about a popular honor student who made a bad decision that had lifelong consequences. It changed people's perception of her. When she walked down the hallway at school, she knew that her reputation had preceded her.

Reputation as defined by dictionary.com is the following:

> *"The estimation in which a person or thing is held, especially by the community or the public generally. It went on to say, reputation, refers to the position one occupies or the standing that one has in the opinion of others, in respect to attainments, integrity and the like."*

Sometimes we worry, and change our behavior based on how we perceive that people see us. In instances like this, reputation is our main concern. We have a public image that we want to maintain. We want people to think that we have it all together even if we don't. So, we say the right things, make the right choices, and smile at the right time in public. This becomes a public persona. People can speak well of you and offer complimentary references about you based on your public image.

Most of us ladies become proficient at an early age at cultivating the image we want to portray to the world. They see the well-practiced smile, the fashionable clothes, on point makeup, and the I-have-it-all-together façade. Hence, they think they know your story.

We all have stories floating around about us. Some are true and some are not. They start early on. It doesn't matter who you are: Christian, non-believer, the so-called good girl or bad girl. People often think they know your story based on looks or reputation.

- If you're quiet, you can be labeled snobby or standoffish.

- If you're loud or talk a lot, you risk being regarded as obnoxious.

- If you're very friendly, you can be perceived as a flirt.

The list goes on and these perceptions can become your reputation. When people hear your name, they already have preconceived notions about you. Reputation is important. The Bible speaks about having a good reputation.

> *"Choose a good reputation over great riches; being held in high esteem is better than silver or gold." - Proverbs 22:1 NLT*

Nothing hurts or makes you as angry as when your reputation is unfairly tarnished. To the degree that you're capable, you try to keep your reputation protected. We all want to have a good reputation and there is nothing wrong with that. I encourage it. Have a reputation for being good, doing good, being honest and kind. However, remember, despite all the good you do to cultivate a good reputation, your reputation can change. Sandra discovered this in the most painful way.

- One wrong choice or even perceived wrong choice can totally wreck a perfectly good reputation.
- One ill thought out action can change your life.
- One conversation, Facebook post, text message, tweet or Instagram post and life as you know it is no more.

The Internet is full of examples of ill thought out actions and comments that ruined reputations and lives. Were these people mean spirited or horrible people as they have been portrayed? I think not. Many of them simply made a mistake. They said the wrong thing to the wrong person, pressed publish when they should have thought twice and now have experienced the embarrassment of having their name under a scrolling headline that says, "***Trending.***"

They know what it means to have a tattered reputation with numerous labels. They are labeled weird, promiscuous, racist, stupid, sexist, etc. Their life in some cases becomes the punchline of a comedian's hurtful jokes. Wherever they go, whether it's to school, job interviews, dates, etc., their reputation precedes them.

Should I Even Fight?

Have you ever asked yourselves the question, "Why should I even bother to fight?" People are going to believe what they want to believe anyway, so why bother? You've had things said about you that wasn't true. You were treated unfairly, left out or made fun of for your mistakes.

Maybe you were on the other side of the spectrum and you were made fun of for your beliefs, called a goodie-two shoe or old fashioned and outdated because of your beliefs and values. Your very good reputation caused you to be ostracized because it made you different. It caused your peers to label you *weird*, *different* or *she thinks she's better than others*. It made you self-conscious and uncomfortable in your own skin. You wondered if you needed to change to fit in with everyone else's mold.

Whatever label you find yourself placed under by others, it isn't easy. Negative or positive, they all sometimes come with a light shining on you, the light and scrutiny of public opinion. Under this harsh light, everyone has a say in your story. The comments never balance out. Just when you have the comfort of feeling as if someone is on your side, someone else's comment leaves you reeling. You struggle trying to makes sense of the commentary because it doesn't match the person you are inside or the person you want to become. You begin to wonder if it is worth the fight to keep going if no one supports you or believes in you.

The answer is *"Yes! My dear girl! Your life, your dreams, your reputation is worth fighting for."* There is Someone who knows your story with all the plots and twists. No matter what the plot of your story is, God's commentary is never condemning or condescending.

You're probably shaking your head in skepticism. You've probably experienced being let down by important people in your life. Friends have possibly shown you that they can't always be trusted. You've most likely not lived up to your own words a few times. These experiences have helped form the conclusion that God is not who He says He is, and He doesn't always live up to His word. So how do you go from skepticism to belief?

You get to know the very heart of God. You can only speak with total assurance on behalf of someone whom you have invested time in getting to know. You know the true nature of this person. You know their character so well that if someone spoke negatively of them in your presence you can immediately defend them simply because you know their heart.

God wants you to know His heart intimately. If you truly get to know His heart, that intimacy will leave you in awe of how He feels about you, what He thinks about you, the destiny He has planned for you. You don't believe me? Let me tell you a Bible story about a woman who everyone had something to say about.

- *If there was Twitter in her day,* it would have been buzzing with tweets about her.
- *If there was a Facebook*, posts about her would have gone viral.
- *If there was Instagram,* her photos would be known worldwide.

Still in the absence of Social Media, her story reached to even the most important and influential people in society. These were the people who had the power to make her life easier or a living nightmare. **They chose the latter.** They sneered at her, judged her and decided her fate based on her present story. In their minds, she would never rise above her current circumstances. She was labeled immoral, meaning she did not conform to the accepted standards of morality.

#Immoral… A little of her story

> *"One of the Pharisees asked Jesus to have dinner with him, so Jesus went to his home and sat down to eat. When **a certain immoral** woman from that city heard he was eating there, she brought a beautiful alabaster jar filled with expensive perfume. Then she knelt behind him at his feet, weeping. Her tears fell on his feet, and she wiped them off with her hair. Then she kept kissing his feet and putting perfume on them." - Luke 7:36-38 (NLT)*

This woman was labeled and shunned because she made choices that caused her what I'm sure was at one time a well cultivated reputation. She wasn't always an immoral, sinful woman. No one becomes that way overnight. I'm sure she had a life before with dreams and plans.

She probably had sleepovers and outings with her friends where they giggled and laughed and made plans much like the young ladies today.

Most likely she dreamed of her Prince Charming coming to sweep her off her feet and carry her off into happily ever after on his beautiful stallion.

Or, perhaps, she aspired to be a shrewd business woman and to take care of herself and her family much like the virtuous woman described in Proverbs 31.

Whether it was due to a traumatic event that left scars on her soul, dysfunctional family circumstances that caused her to grow up too fast, or bad choices that spiraled out of control, somewhere along the way the precocious schoolgirl, the giggling, idealistic teen stopped dreaming.

The beautiful dreams she had for her future began to shatter one by one until finally she had nothing left to hold on to. Hence, she gave up on herself and her dreams.

She listened to the dream killers, whether they were outward or inward, and decided that her dreams were not worth fighting for, waiting for or believing for anymore. She listened and she decided to settle for simply existing and continuously living down to her reputation, trapped by other people's perception of her and her own bad choices.

What's your story?

Like this woman, I'm sure you have a reputation. **We all do**.

Perhaps you feel lonely, misunderstood and unloved.

Maybe you have a secret you'd like to share, but you're afraid you'll be condemned or made fun of.

Perhaps you played around in high school and dropped out without a diploma.

Maybe you said yes to sex prematurely and it resulted in you becoming a mother before you were an adult.

Maybe you gave into peer pressure and took what you thought would be just one drink of alcohol and now you find yourself sneaking a drink on a regular basis.

Or maybe you find yourself simply going through the motions of living with no joy, no plans or goals for the future. You don't even know what your story is.

Can I ask you another question? Who are you listening to?

Have you allowed the opinions of others to cause you to lose hope in having a bright future? Have you decided that you've messed up so much in life that you can't possibly accomplish your dreams? Are you allowing others to write the end to your story when you have so much more in life that you can accomplish? I know, that's more than one question. I hope you think about the answers.

You don't have to share your story until you're ready. I challenge you today to learn from this woman you're going to read about who was labeled immoral, cast aside and shunned. (We'll learn more about her in the next chapter.) Don't stay where you are wishing things would change and that the people who rejected you and wrote you off will suddenly accept you. *Work through the pain!* Do something to get from where you are now to someplace better.

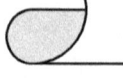

Dear Friend,

*The topic of this chapter is one I always want you to remember. Your reputation precedes you! Often before people get to know you, they know **of** you.*

You may have a good reputation or you may have made choices that have caused your reputation to suffer. If the latter is true, remember that you don't have to walk with your head permanently hung down.

In this chapter you were introduced to a woman who had a horrible reputation. In fact, she was shunned by her community because of the choices she made.

As you continue reading you will see how this woman found hope in Jesus.

Guess what? You can too.

Praying for you,

Bernadine

Time to Think!

*You are now half way through this book. You should be extremely proud of yourself. Time for a little doodling break... so doodle **your proud face**, add a border, some color, get ready to think...*

Shh... Secret Fact
about your quest companion

Confession.... I doodle because, at times, I have a short attention span....

Questions to Think About

1. What is reputation?

2. Proverbs 22:1 states, *"Choose a good reputation over great riches; being held in high esteem is better than silver or gold." (NLT)* Explain why reputation is so important.

3. Explain how someone's reputation can be ruined.

4. In the story at the beginning of the chapter, Sandra, a popular honor student, made a choice that had lifelong consequences. Describe a time you made a choice that affected your reputation negatively.

5. The woman from the Bible reading in this chapter was labeled immoral and sinful. Describe a time you felt that you were living under a label that someone had placed on you. How did it affect you?

6. Whatever label you find yourself placed under by others isn't easy. Negative or positive, all labels come with a light shining on you, the light and scrutiny of public opinion. Do you think these statements are true? Why? Why not?

7. The negative impact that Social Media can have is emphasized in this chapter. Have you ever pressed share on a Social Media post and thought, "*Oh no?*" Share your story.

8. What is a lesson you've learned from a mistake you've made?

9. If you were asked to memorize a Bible verse quoted in this chapter, which verse would it be and why?

10. Write a note to Sandra, the girl in the story at the beginning of this chapter. Tell her about a time you made a mistake and how you got past it. Encourage her not to give up.

Chapter 6
Get Up and Get Moving

"Do something today that your future self will thank you for." -Anonymous

Would you find it difficult to go to a party that you weren't invited to and you knew you would not be welcomed? If you were bold enough to go to the party, are you brave enough to walk up and monopolize the attention of the guest of honor? In this chapter, you'll learn more about the woman who decided that she wanted something badly enough that she would be courageous enough to go after it, even in the face of hostility and opposition.

> *"When **a certain immoral** woman from that city heard he was eating there, she brought a beautiful alabaster jar filled with expensive perfume. Then she knelt behind him at his feet, weeping." - Luke 7:37-38 (NLT)*

One day this woman who had been labeled immoral decided to seek the teacher she had heard so much about. It's obvious from the passage that she desired change from the way she was living. She made a conscious decision to step out of her situation and move towards something better. For one moment, she let go of what others thought about her and gatecrashed a party to seek out Jesus.

She did not know if Jesus would condemn her or label her like everyone else did, but He was her last hope. She wanted change so badly that she refused to let fear of rejection hold her back. But, even as she knelt at His feet, there were accusatory stares, whispers and labels.

> *"When the Pharisee who had invited him saw this, he said to himself, 'If this man were a prophet, he would know what kind of woman is touching him. She's a sinner!'" - Luke 7:39 (NIV)*

Unfortunately, there are people who will characterize you by information they know about you. They refuse to believe that you can grow and transform into a better version of yourself. Some people find a certain sense of satisfaction in letting others know your past mistakes and refuse to let you forget them. Whenever you try to move beyond it, they are quick to remind you. In their minds, you are always supposed to walk with your head hung down, forever ashamed by your sins and shunned because of your mistakes.

We don't know anything about this woman before this. All we know about her is her negative reputation that preceded her. We know that she was perceived to be an immoral, sinful woman who was not worth Jesus' time

"I wish I had made different choices," she said to me, head hung down. "What do you mean?" I asked because we were just chatting, not talking about anything serious.

She didn't respond, just continued what she was doing, so I said to her, "Do you know that none of the decisions you made in your life, even the ones you considered your biggest mistakes, surprise God?"

She stopped and waited for me to go on. I shared the following verse with her: **"You saw me before I was born. Every day of my life was recorded in your book. Every moment was laid out before a single day had passed." - Psalm 139:16 (NLT)**

We've all probably wondered a time or two, "Did I make decisions that threw my life off the course God set for me?" Don't despair. Nothing that happens in your life is a surprise to God. Our life story was written in His book before we were even conceived.

He knew every decision we were going to make and He had a plan in place for when we didn't choose His predestined path. The place you're at in life is not your final destination. There is still more that you are capable of and still more that God has planned for you if you would just trust Him with your heart and your life.

At the end of our conversation she said to me, "I think I need to keep a copy of that verse so I can read it daily and let it sink in." I was only too happy to make a bookmark with the verse on it as a gift to her. I made one for myself too as a reminder that there is nothing about me that God doesn't already know and He loves me just the same.

Often when you make wrong choices, there are people who will suddenly forget all the good that you did before. If you allow them the power, your life will become more about your mistakes than who you are. The Bible says that all have sinned and fallen short of God's glory (Romans 3:23). Everyone who has walked this earth, except for Jesus Christ Himself, has made mistakes. Some have made bad or sometimes horrible life changing choices. *We must be aware, though, that our choices do come with consequences.* Even when we are sorry and repentant, we still often must bear the consequences for the choices we make. However, no one is beyond the hope of God's forgiveness should she ask. *Even if you have made choices that society, friends or family labeled unforgivable, there is Someone who always sees beyond the label.*

- Jesus considers your heart, and He says you are worth more than the mistake.

- You are worth more than the thoughtless words you blurted out in anger or ignorance.

- You are worth more than the Facebook post that should never have been shared.

- You are worth more than the tweet that should never have been tweeted or retweeted.

- My dear young lady, you are worth more than the Instagram photo that should never have been shared or the video that went viral.

You are far more precious than those bad choices that are now permanent, frozen moments in time for the world to view, read and replay at their leisure. They may determine these things to be unforgivable, but **don't believe the lie. You are not the sum of your mistakes.**

Are you walking with your head hung down because of bad choices you have made?

When this woman met Jesus, her head was hung down because she knew her reputation had preceded her. She probably thought He would reject her just like everyone else. She carried with her the hurtful memories of those who passed her on the street and turned their heads, those who abandoned her, whispered behind their hands when they saw her, the former friends who no longer met her eyes because they knew who she was.

To them she was beyond hope. They treated her as if she carried some nameless but highly contagious disease. What would be Jesus' response?

A New Label… Forgiven

> *"Then Jesus said to the woman, 'Your sins are forgiven.'" - Luke 7:48 (NLT)*

Instant forgiveness. No explanations or excuses necessary. Just total love and acceptance. *I promise you dear reader, when you seek out Jesus, He will not reject you.* He will not inflict more wounds on an already hurting and scarred soul.

The woman with the alabaster box sought Jesus because she was tired of the life she was living. This woman realized that she could become more than she was at that moment. She was in search of something only Jesus could give. *A new label.* Jesus did not disappoint her. His response soothed the sting of the whispers and stares. It renewed her hope and her belief in her dreams and her future.

When you have an encounter with Jesus, you come out knowing that you are loved and that your life is not over; it still has meaning. This woman had an encounter with Jesus that transformed her life. It erased the negative labels. He remembered them no more. They no longer had the power to hold her back. She was free to be all that He had created her to be. She was transformed by His grace.

While we may not have a public label such as immoral, sinful or unforgivable, all of us like this woman have made wrong choices. We have also experienced the sting of rejection, whispers and stares. Just like her, we too can come to Jesus. After reading this woman's story, I imagined myself coming to Jesus and was inspired to write the following poem. Maybe you'll see yourself in it also.

Like the Woman with the Alabaster Box...I Came

Like the woman with the alabaster box,
I came to Jesus.
I came to Him with emotional baggage of many kinds
but still, I came.
I came with the residue of pain from past hurts,
I couldn't let go.
I came to Him knowing that
many had written me off,
Wondering if Jesus would see something
worth saving in me.
Hopefully, I came.
But as I knelt before Him,
something happened.
The Lamb of God, savior of the world
reached down and lifted me to my feet.
He took my chin within His hand and
lifted my face towards His own.
In his eyes I saw such kindness,
compassion and love.
I wept.
He dried my tears and called me by name.
"My child, weep no more I am here," He said.
As I looked into His eyes, I continued to weep
and as I wept, my burdens...
They miraculously disappeared
the pain,
the hurt,
the shame...
I felt it no more
Like the woman with the alabaster box,
when I left His presence
I was rejoicing
I was forgiven
I was free

*"Be more concerned with your character than
your reputation, because your character is what
you really are, while your reputation is merely
what others think you are." - John Wooden*

My dear girl, your reputation may precede you, but you don't have to let it define you. It's not too late to become the person you want to be. It just takes some work and commitment on your part. I promise you, it's worth it. So as we continue this quest, we will be looking at the importance of building your character in a positive way.

Dear Friend,

You are precious to God!

You are not the sum of your mistakes. You can make choices that bring about new changes in your life and reputation. An encounter with Jesus can totally transform your life!

So, do what the lady with the alabaster box did. **Get up and get moving***. Take the actions that will bring about positive changes in your life.*

Remember also that in our technology driven world, it is almost impossible to live a life sheltered from prying eyes and ears. So make good choices on Social Media. **Before you press publish or send, stop and think.**

I believe in you! I don't want you to give up on yourself or your dreams. Let's put some new labels in place; let the trending topic be Transformed by His Amazing Grace #new creation #forgiven #God's girl

Cheering you on,

Bernadine

Time to Think!

You're doing great! The doodling must be working, so ... **doodle on, draw a border, add some color, get ready to think...**

Shh... Secret Fact
about your quest companion

I question God at times, but I never regret giving my heart to Him.

Questions to Think About

1. Why do you think the "immoral woman" decided to go see Jesus?

2. What happened when she knelt at Jesus' feet?

3. What did Jesus say to the woman?

4. How do you think the woman's life changed after her encounter with Jesus?

5. How would an encounter like this change your life?

6. Have you ever felt as if you didn't belong somewhere because you were different in some way? Explain.

7. Have you ever wondered if decisions you made were unforgivable? Explain.

8. What is one takeaway from this chapter that will remain with you?

9. If you were asked to memorize a Bible verse quoted in this chapter, which verse would it be and why?

10. Finish the following note to God:

Dear God,

I've made a few mistakes in my life that often cause me to walk with my head hung down. Now, after reading this chapter, I have hope that...

Chapter 7
Character Matters

"The final forming of a person's character lies in their own hands."
- Anne Frank

I was watching an episode of "Project Runway Junior" when I first heard the term *OOTD*. I wasn't quite sure what it meant so I googled it. If there's the least bit of a possibility that you are as uninformed as I was, I included the definition for you.

According to slangdefinition.com OOTD means:

"Outfit of the Day, a very popular acronym and hashtag on Instagram, and used often on Facebook, Twitter, Tumblr, and other Social Media websites and apps. People will add the hashtag OOTD to photos of their outfits on any given day. The tag is usually used on photos posted by people who like their outfit and want to share it with others."

When people use the hashtag, it's usually because they feel good about their choice of outfit that day and they want to share it with others. No one from what I can see posts a deliberately unflattering photo of themselves for the world to see.

We do the same with our character traits. We often put the best on display when we are being observed and we suppress those that are negative. We want to be seen in a positive light. However, just as an unflattering photo sometimes gets mixed in with those OOTD posts, so does some of the not so nice things about a person's character also become public.

The previous chapter focused on the impact of reputation. There are people who hide behind a spotless reputation for long periods of time. However, if their character doesn't match their reputation, it will eventually become public knowledge.

The Internet has countless stories of people whose reputations were ruined when it was made public that their private lives didn't match their public facades. They found out the hard way that a carefully cultivated, spotless reputation that masks a privately dishonest or immoral character is meaningless.

According to Miriam Webster dictionary: *"character is, the way someone thinks, feels, and behaves: someone's personality."*

Character is built and developed choice by choice, day by day. Every decision you make contributes to the building of your character. So, work on consistently making the choices that will help you to build your character in a positive way. This process of character building is essential because *although God loves you and accepts you just as you are, He doesn't expect you to remain in the same condition you were in when you gave your heart to Him.* When you accept Jesus into your heart, something must change. You should be constantly evaluating yourself and allowing His transforming work to be done in your life. After all, you're becoming the best possible version of yourself that you can be.

Be aware though that you cannot change yourself. It is only Jesus who can bring lifelong, positive changes in your life. So, as you continue your quest to becoming the girl of His dreams, you must continuously work on building your character with the aim of becoming more like Him.

A Few Basic Steps to Building your Character

1. **Be a girl who reads the Bible and prays.**

Prayer and Bible reading were discussed in detail in the previous chapters. Both are equally important when you decide to actively pursue developing your character in a positive manner. As you read the Bible, it helps you develop a clear picture of who God is and what He expects of you. His Word gives you a guideline to live by that will help you grow into the best version of yourself that you can be.

> *"How can a young person stay on the path of purity? By living according to your word."*
> *- Psalm 119:9 NIV*

As you read God's Word, pray about the areas in your life that you want to change. Ask Him to help you to live your life according to His word. That's what I did as a Christian teen. I saw character traits in the lives of the men and women I read about in the Bible that I wanted to emulate. I began to pray to God for the same qualities I wanted to develop in my life. I wanted to use their lives as a pattern to develop my character. You can do the same as you read His Word. For example, I prayed for the following character traits:

- ***Courage*** like Esther, to be willing to do scary things in spite of my fears.
- ***Loyalty*** like Ruth, who was loyal and devoted to the people in her life.
- ***Determination*** like Nehemiah, who never gave up but completed his task despite the difficulties.
- ***Integrity*** like Joseph, who did not compromise his values although it meant going to prison.
- ***Humility*** like David, who when he made mistakes was swift to repent.

These are just a few examples of the biblical characters I admire. You can find countless more as you read your Bible. Positive changes in character, however, doesn't come through prayer alone. Work must be done also.

You develop courage by taking opportunities to do things that scare you instead of letting them stop you.

You develop integrity by consistently doing the right thing even if it goes against what everyone else is doing.

2. **Be a girl of your word.**

My word is my bond! This is a saying that was common when I was growing up. It was used most often when someone was being questioned as to whether she would keep her word. By saying, *My word is my bond,* she simply meant that she could be trusted to keep her promise.

Are you a girl of your word? Can you be trusted to do the things you say you're going to do?

In the verses below, Jesus tells a parable about a father and two sons.

> *"There was a man who had two sons. He went to the first and said, 'Son, go and work today in the vineyard.' 'I will not,' he answered, but later he changed his mind and went. Then the father went to the other son and said the same thing. He answered, 'I will, sir,' but he did not go." - Matthew 21:28-31 (NIV)*

Which of these sons do you think the father was pleased with? The one who promised the father that he would complete a task but didn't or the one who said no in the beginning but later changed his mind and did what his father wanted? It's easy to make promises because you don't want to say no and be perceived as an unkind person. However, if you repeatedly break your word, no one will believe you when you make a promise. They will then begin to question whether you can be depended upon to keep your word.

3. **Be a girl of integrity.**

> *"Whoever walks in integrity walks securely, but whoever takes crooked paths will be found out."*
> *- Proverbs 10:9 (NIV)*

According to Cambridge dictionary, "*integrity is the quality of being honest and having strong moral principles that you refuse to change.*" Hence, to be considered a girl of integrity you must consistently behave according to the moral values that you believe in. To do this, you must first know what your moral values are based on God's Word. Also, you must set boundaries for yourself that you strive not to cross. Make your boundaries known and teach others to respect them.

For example, suppose you're in a group study session with some of your classmates. One of them pulls out the answer key to the test that you're going to take the next day. Everyone else in the group seems happy to look at the answer key, relieved that they are going to pass the test. However, you know that this is cheating. Do you speak up and risk being ostracized? Or do you quietly go along even though you know it's the wrong thing to do?

The above is just one scenario. There are countless other scenarios in every area of life that you may find yourself faced with. Your constant choice to do the right thing is what helps you to become a person of integrity. With God's help, you can consistently make those right choices. Pray and ask Him to give you the strength to make the right choice when you are faced with the decision between doing something right and something wrong.

4. Be a girl who choses her friends wisely.

Have you ever noticed that when you spend a lot of time with certain friends you take on some of their mannerisms? You may talk like them or repeat some of the same phrases or even do some of the same things without even thinking about it. This is one of the reasons why it is important to choose your friends wisely. "

> *"Do not be misled: 'Bad company corrupts good character.'" - 1 Corinthians 15:33(NIV)*

From this verse, we can surmise that character can be influenced by the people that you are surrounded by just like your daily outfits can be influenced by seasons and fashion trends. If the people who you are around most consistently display negative attitudes and character traits in their speech and actions, it's easy to take on those same traits and attitudes. Little by little you may find yourself changing who you are to fit in with your friends. So, be mindful of the friends who hold places of influence in your life. Ensure that you have similar values and that you are prompting each other to make choices that will build and develop your character in a positive way.

5. **Be a girl who repents.**

Being a Christian isn't always easy. The truth is, *despite your best effort, there are days when you will stumble and fall short.* I think this is one of the reasons why David is one of my favorite biblical characters. He is an excellent example of someone who messed up in a huge way.

I remember reading Psalm 51 and wondering what had happened to make David write these heartfelt words.

> *"Have mercy on me, O God, according to your unfailing love; according to your great compassion blot out my transgressions. Wash away all my iniquity and cleanse me from my sin." - Psalm 51:1-2 (NIV)*

So, I looked for the back story which begins in 2 Samuel chapter 11. David had sinned by committing adultery with Bathsheba, the wife of Uriah, one of his soldiers. After Bathsheba became pregnant, David arranged for Uriah to be killed in battle to cover it up. (Sounds like a plot from a soap opera, doesn't it?) God was very displeased with David's actions and sent the prophet Nathan to warn him. After Nathan had spoken to him, David saw how selfish he had been and the damage his selfish actions had done to his relationship with God. It was after this that David wrote Psalm 51.

You can sense David's sincerity as he pours out his heart to God. He didn't make excuses for his sins. David accepted responsibility for his actions and repented as illustrated in the following verses.

> *"Create in me a pure heart, O God, and renew a steadfast spirit within me. Do not cast me from your presence or take your Holy Spirit from me." - Psalm 51:10-11 (NIV)*

God wants you to do the same as David did. Go before Him with a repentant heart when you sin. Real repentance comes from the heart. It is a genuine commitment to change the sinful behavior and refrain from doing it again. When you sin, it causes separation between you and God and only true repentance can restore the relationship back to its original state.

Something to Think About

The Apostle Paul discusses some character traits that all Christians should display. They are known as the fruit of the spirit.

> *"But the Holy Spirit produces this kind of fruit in our lives: love, joy, peace, patience, kindness, goodness, faithfulness, gentleness, and self-control." - Galatians 5:22-23 (NLT)*

Are you displaying the Fruit of the Spirit in your life? Would the people who know you best agree that they have seen them on display in your words and actions? Would they say that you are kind and dependable? Would they agree that you practice self-control even when it's difficult to do so?

As you come to the end of this chapter, I'd like to remind you that building your character is an ongoing process. It is a daily walk of making the choices that cause you to grow into the person you want to be. Character building sometimes comes down to simple decisions and actions such as:

- The way you talk to and about people.

- The way you treat others.

- The people you surround yourself with.

- The way you react to different situations.

- The way you take responsibility for your actions.

- How consistent you are in developing your relationship with Jesus Christ.

Take a minute and evaluate yourself.

Are you the girl of His dreams?

Have you given Him your heart?

Are you getting to know Him?

Are you allowing Him to help you build your character?

As you read your Bible, you'll notice that even Jesus' life was one of constant growth. His life is the perfect example to follow as you continue your quest of development.

> *"Jesus grew in wisdom and in stature and in favor with God and all the people." - Luke 2:52 (NLT)*

I promise you, the time you put into developing your character and allowing God to transform you is not wasted time. *You will **never** regret it because the girl of His dream grows into the woman He created her to be.*

Dear Friend,

The topic of character is such a huge one that it is impossible to do it justice in such a short chapter. There are many facets of character, and it's up to you to decide by your words, actions and attitude how you want your character to be.

If you were to honestly describe your own character, what are some of the character traits that you would list? Would the words honest, trustworthy, loyal, hardworking, kind, dependable... be included in the list?

Remember, **your story is still being written and it's up to you to decide the type of person you want to become.** *You won't get it right all the time but keep going.* **Use your triumphs to inspire you and your mistakes to propel you.**

Don't allow what others think about you to stop you from becoming the best you that you can be.

Find inspiration in the Bible to help you to grow into the person you want to become.

Let's grow together,

Bernadine

Time to Think!

Wow! You've come so far… Don't get tired now. Doodle a picture of something that resonated with you in this chapter or simply, **add some color, get ready to think...**

Shh... Secret Fact
about your quest companion

As a teenager I wanted to be a fashion designer, although I couldn't draw…

Questions to Think About

1. Define character. How is character different from reputation?

2. Who is responsible for the forming of one's character?

3. What do you think is meant by the saying, *What is done in the dark will come to light?*

4. How is character building something that is ongoing?

5. How can your character be influenced by friends?

6. What does it mean to be a girl of your word?

7. What are some of the character traits that all Christians should have?

8. Name a biblical character that you admire. What traits did he/she have that you would like to see in your life?

9. What do you think is your best character trait? Explain why you chose that one.

10. Finish the following note to God:

Dear God,

As I read Your Word, I am inspired by the life of some of the people I'm reading about. I want to develop some of their character traits in my life...

Section Four
The Transformation

Life Lessons from a butterfly

Let go of the past
Trust the future
Embrace change
Come out of the cocoon
Unfurl your wings
Dare to get off the ground
Ride the breezes
Savor the flowers
Put on your brightest colors
Let your beauty show
(Author Unknown)

"And be not conformed to this world: but be ye transformed by the renewing of your mind, that ye may prove what is that good, and acceptable, and perfect, will of God." - Romans 12:2 (KJV)

Chapter 8
Letting Go and Moving Forward

"Just when the caterpillar thought the world was over, it became a butterfly." -Anonymous

I love a good makeover show, don't you? Makeovers can be as simple as a new hairstyle and makeup, wardrobe changes, or as complicated as cosmetic surgery. In my opinion, the best ones always have a lot of angst and drama as the person getting the makeover reluctantly lets go of her old habits. Sometimes tears are shed as the clothes that represent the old life are tossed into the garbage bin.

Often, the person being made over wants to hold on to the old unstylish, worn out outfits even though she knows that she is going to receive something better. Who wouldn't want to let go of a closet full of old clothes and purchase a new wardrobe on someone else's dime?

Unfortunately, people get into a routine and the old way of dressing and doing things become a habit. They become as familiar as an old fuzzy blanket or favorite pair of jeans that you don't want to let go of no matter how tattered and torn it is.

Case and point, when I started writing this book, I was a single lady living in my own home with things around me that I loved. I had no plans to get rid of any of it, especially my books. However, a tall, handsome, brown eyed guy came into my life when I least expected it. He traveled thousands of miles to the Bahamas, got down on one knee and asked me to marry him.

I said, *"Yes!"*

And so it began... the process of saying goodbye to all that was familiar to me. In order to move forward, I had to pack up my home and move to a new country. It took me months of packing, unpacking, repacking and lots of tears before I was satisfied with what I felt was important enough to carry into my new life. The hardest part was letting go of things that I once thought were very important. In fact, in one conversation I told my fiancé, "Love me, love my books. We come as a package deal."

I simply wasn't hearing his, "You can build a new library." It had taken me years to build up my book collection. Some of my books dated back to when I was a teenager. They meant a lot to me and I couldn't imagine calling someplace home without my books. I hadn't figured out how I would ship hundreds of books along with other important stuff, but I didn't intend to leave them behind.

> *"See, I will do a new thing. It will begin happening now. Will you not know about it? I will even make a road in the wilderness, and rivers in the desert." - Isaiah 43:19 (NIV)*

It took me a while, but I finally came to the realization that I don't have to hold on to everything that I loved. I didn't have to take everything from my old life into my new life. *Some things serve their time and then you must let them go to make way for new blessings that God wants to bring into your life.* When this finally clicked in my head, I made progress with my packing. In fact, I did it with a joyful heart and felt my heart getting lighter as I shed the things I already knew were not realistic for me to take with me as I began a new chapter in my life.

Are you wondering why I place emphasis on my books instead of clothes since I began by talking about makeovers? *It's because they were what were hardest for me to let go of.* I think my fiancé realized how much I loved him the day I sent him a photo of my library with stacks of books on the floor waiting to go to the new homes I had found for them. It signaled that I was leaving the baggage behind and moving toward our new life together.

> *"No, dear brothers, I am still not all I should be, but I am bringing all my energies to bear on this one thing: Forgetting the past and looking forward to what lies ahead." -* Philippians 3:13 (TLB)

Do you know what the word *metamorphosis* means? I'm sure you've learned about it in your primary school science class. It is *the process of transformation from an immature form to an adult form.* The butterfly, for example, has to let go of the safety of its cocoon in order to completely transform and move forward. I'm sure it's difficult to leave the safety of the cocoon but once it does, the butterfly never looks back. It embraces its new life.

What would you say is the hardest thing for you to let go of? Think about it as you continue this quest we're on. Becoming God's dream girl is the ultimate makeover. It's a transformation from the inside out. To achieve this transformation, you must let go of the baggage that holds you back. I'm not referring to physical baggage, like hundreds of books or closet full of shoes, bags and clothes.

We all carry baggage that is not visible to people around us. Two of the main obstacles that can hold you back from moving forward in life are the following:

- Holding onto past hurts and unforgiveness.
- Holding onto falsehoods that you believe about yourself.

The Baggage of Unforgiveness

Her: "I'm not your friend!"

Me: "What?"

Her: "I'm not your friend!"

I could barely keep the smile off my face as I looked down into the pouting face of my cute, two-year old goddaughter. She was quite angry with me and not afraid to show it. The fact that we were in church and she was sitting on my lap at the time did not impress her at all. The sweetest thing, however, was that two minutes later she earnestly looked at me and said, ***"I am your friend."*** *Just like that I was forgiven.*

Many girls have deep wounds and hurts that they don't tell anyone about. Someone hurts you whether by something they say or do. You keep it bottled up inside unwilling to let it go and forgive the person even if he or she asks for forgiveness. Have you ever noticed how easily children forgive? Somehow, we lose either the ability or desire to easily forgive as we get older. Jesus tells us however:

> *"Truly I tell you, unless you change and become like little children, you will never enter the kingdom of heaven." - Matthew 18:3 (NIV)*

Little children make the act of forgiveness seem so easy, almost effortless. However, forgiveness can be one of the most difficult things to do, especially when someone hurts you and refuses to acknowledge that they wronged you. During your lifetime, you will be hurt and offended many times. People, including your family and friends, will hurt you. You're human so you'll undoubtedly be angry, but how long do you stay angry?

I find that many times ladies are experts at holding grudges (I speak from experience). Someone wounds you and you hold on to the pain and refuse to let it go. Every time you see the person, you get angrier and angrier because you keep remembering what they did to you or said about you. Unfortunately, holding the grudge causes you more pain because it gives the person the power to hurt you over and over again.

There are times you may feel that you have a valid reason not to forgive. A horrendous act may have been committed against you. It may even take you a while to get to the place where you feel you're able to genuinely forgive. One part of the Lord's prayer reads: *"Forgive us our trespasses as we forgive those who trespasses against us"* (Matthew 6.12). As difficult as it may be to do, the terms of forgiveness (as laid out in the Bible) are not negotiable. *If we want to be forgiven, we must also forgive.*

Pray about it and ask God to give you a forgiving heart. Allow Him to heal the wounds. Let Him help you to let go of the heavy burden of unforgiveness and hurts from the past. Only then will you fully experience His transforming process in your life.

Transformation can be a painful process, but you cannot grow and change into the person that God desires for you to be unless you are willing to take inventory of your life periodically and discard the things that are simply taking up space and hindering you from moving forward.

Falsehoods We Believe

Another obstacle that can hold you back from embracing your new life in Christ and allowing His work in you to be fully realized, may be feelings of inadequacy and the falsehoods that you tell yourself or believe about yourself. You may think:

- I'm not good enough.
- I'm not brave enough.
- I'm not smart enough.
- I'm not pretty enough.
- I'm not rich enough.
- I'm not athletic enough.
- I don't speak well enough.
- I'm not _____ enough

Many people have felt this way including some of my biblical heroes. Can I share something with you? *God often does His best transformation in the lives of those who didn't think they were enough but who opened their hearts and lives to Him anyway.*

Once such person I'm reminded of is Gideon. Gideon's story starts in Judges chapter 6. When you're first introduced to Gideon, he is living a defeated life. He has a low self-esteem and like many of us he doesn't think he is enough. Gideon was approached by the angel of God, who said to him in verse 12: *"The Lord is with you, mighty warrior."*

At that moment, Gideon felt nothing like a warrior. In fact, he felt like a nobody. He couldn't see in himself what God saw in him. God saw a mighty warrior, but Gideon saw himself as the runt of the litter, the least in his father's house. In verse 15 he asked God, "*How can I save Israel? My clan is the weakest in Manasseh, and I am the least in my family.*"

Wow! Talk about low self-esteem. His clan was the weakest and he was the least in his clan. That's like a double whammy! You can't get much lower than that.

Like Gideon you may see yourself as less than you are. But God doesn't! He knows what you are capable of. He sees the you He created you to be. He still has a future planned for you and wants you to become the person that you are meant to be.

> *"For we are God's masterpiece. He has created us anew in Christ Jesus, so we can do the good things he planned for us long ago."   - Ephesians 2:10 (NLT)*

Gideon wanted to be sure that God had indeed called him so he asked for a sign. God gave Gideon the sign just as he asked so Gideon went back to his army and prepared to face the Midianites. However, God told him that his army of tens of thousands was too large. *Sometimes you may feel braver or more capable when you're a part of a large group or have a wide support system. But what do you do when they're not available?* God wanted Gideon to know that the battle wouldn't be won because of the large army but because He was with Gideon. In the end, Gideon was left with 300 men to defeat the Midianites.

It was at night when Gideon called his men to go to battle. He gave each of them empty pitchers with torches inside and trumpets. He then led them to the enemy camp. He divided the men into three groups and they went and surrounded the Midianites' camp. Then they blew their trumpets and broke their pitchers, so that the lights shone out. Then they each shouted, "*The sword of* the Lord and of Gideon!" The Midianites turned against each other in confusion, and Gideon won an easy victory. God proved to Gideon that when you trust in Him, *you can achieve more than you think you are capable of with less than you thought possible.*

Gideon allowed God's vision of him to wipe out the vision he had of himself. At the end of chapter 7 in Judges, the defeated Gideon we met in chapter 6 has vanished. By the end of chapter 7, he is now the mighty warrior that the angel had called him in chapter 6. From a weakling to a leader of men, Gideon had moved far beyond his self-imposed limitations. God had indeed called him by the right name although he couldn't see it at the time. Although God saw Gideon as a mighty warrior, Gideon still had to let go of the picture he had of himself as the runt of the litter.

How do you think God sees you?

Start to see a different you than you are seeing right now. Begin to work on becoming the person God wants you to be. Ask Him to help you to see yourself as He sees you. Let His vision of you wipe out the vision you have of yourself, just like it did for Gideon.

In a makeover show, when the person who is being made over looks in the mirror and gets a first glance at herself, she often wonders why it took so long to decide to make a change. Could she have been the beautiful reflection in the mirror all along if she had just let go of the old and moved on to the new? What about you? *Are you His dream girl or are you still clinging to the past image that represents the girl you used to be?*

It's easy to cling to the image of who you used to be in a world that rarely lets you forget. However, if you've accepted Jesus into your heart, that old picture is no longer an image of who you truly are. He doesn't see you like you used to be.

That image of you is gone.

> *"When someone becomes a Christian, he becomes a brand new person inside. He is not the same anymore. A new life has begun!"* - 2 Corinthians 5:17 (TLB)

Sometimes I've watched makeover shows and thought to myself, she doesn't look that different. However, the person looks in the mirror and is excited by the change she sees and ultimately that's what's important.

As you begin to grow, change and become the person you want to be, people around you may not notice the changes right away. Don't let that cause you to doubt yourself. It's not a race to the finish line. It's a lifelong journey. Just keep moving forward. Keep striving to please God. Spend time reading His word and getting to know Him intimately.

> *"All Scripture is inspired by God and is useful to teach us what is true and to make us realize what is wrong in our lives. It corrects us when we are wrong and teaches us to do what is right. God uses it to prepare and equip his people to do every good work."* - 2 Timothy 3:16-17 (NLT)

Keep the above verses in mind and allow God's Word to become a pattern for your life as it teaches and corrects you. If you allow His Word to become a real consistent part of your life, you will begin to transform. Eventually, the people around you will notice the change in your life. When they do, you'll be able to share with them that a relationship with Jesus Christ made all the difference.

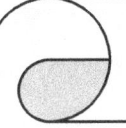

Dear Friend,

What is something that you love that makes you smile?

For me it's butterflies. I love looking at their beautiful, colorful wings. They seem so graceful as they flitter from flower to flower with seemingly not a care in the world. In looking at the beauty of the butterfly, it's easy to forget that it had to go through a transformation to become the beautiful creature that we gaze at and admire. The stunning butterfly was once a fat wriggling caterpillar.

The caterpillar probably didn't know all it could become but **God, the Creator always knew***.*

On the days when the caterpillar crawled on the leaf and looked at the butterflies flying around it, **God knew its future***.*

On the days when the caterpillar was in the darkness of its cocoon, **God knew its destiny.**

And on the day it let go of its cocoon, transformation completed, spread its beautiful wings and took its first flight, **God was not surprised.** *He knew all along what the caterpillar would become.*

My dear young lady, you are no different. Just as God knew the caterpillar would transform into a butterfly; Just as He knew there was a mighty warrior inside the weakling that Gideon saw himself as; He knows that there is greatness inside of you.

So, my friend, let go of those things that are holding you back. Become who He has predestined you to be... His transformed girl.

God's transformed girl,

Bernadine

Time to Think!

You did it!... You are now at the final set of questions (although not quite the end of the book.). Doodle an emoji of how you feel right now, sketch the outfit you're wearing or simply, **add some color, get ready to think***...*

Shh... Secret Fact
about your quest companion

I'm hoping you'll spill a random, silly secret so I don't feel all alone.

Questions to Think About

1. Why do you think it's so hard to let go of things?

2. Explain how unforgiveness can hinder your progress in life?

3. Why do you think children find it so easy to forgive?

4. List three negative beliefs you hold about yourself.

5. How can the beliefs (listed above), negatively affect your growth? How can you change these beliefs?

6. Define transformation in your own words.

7. Why do you think God chose Gideon?

8. By the end of the chapter, Gideon was totally transformed. *How has God changed your life?*

9. Write your name in the blank space of the following paraphrased verse. How does this verse help you to let go of the old image you have of yourself?

> *When _____ becomes a Christian, (she) becomes a brand new person inside.* ***(She)*** *is not the same anymore. A new life has begun!*
> *2 Corinthians 5:17 (TLB)*

10. Finish the following note to God:

Dear God,

I know that I can become more than I am right now. I admit there are some things I must let go of to transform into the person you want me to be...

Final Thoughts

My Dear Young Lady,

It's been a pleasure writing this book for you. I hope you enjoy reading it and feel inspired to become all that God has created you to be. By the way, this dream girl thing, it doesn't mean everyday you're going to be perfect or you're going to always get it right. In fact, just as you begin to feel that you've got everything down pat you're probably going to mess up in some way.

Don't give up! *We all mess up. The Bible says none is perfect. But it also encourages us to strive for perfection. The secret to those you see before you who have been on this journey for years is that they didn't give up.*

So, my dear young lady, I've shared my heart with you because I was you. The shy insecure teen, the one with the self-esteem issues, the one who hid her pain and insecurities sometimes behind a smile, a laugh, a false sense of self confidence. I'm also the girl who tried desperately to become the girl of His dreams. I never gave up even on the days I failed completely.

Today, I can say that He has transformed my life. This little book that you're reading is over 8 years in the making. I should be embarrassed to say that, but I'm not. The dream of publishing this book was important enough that I kept coming back to it and now you're reading it.

I hope this encourages you to keep trying. Keep believing, and get up when you fall. *Below are a few statements I wrote years ago when I first published my teen girl magazine. I wanted to share them with you because they are still true today.*

I believe that all young ladies have the potential to be women of excellent character and integrity and positive contributors to their communities.

I believe we should place more emphasis on the positive things young ladies are involved with instead of the negative.

I believe that even though a young lady may have made mistakes, it's never too late for her to start over and make positive choices.

I believe that we can inspire young ladies to become women of excellence by living transparent lives before them, admitting that we all make mistakes, encouraging them to learn from their mistakes, and most importantly, introducing them to Jesus Christ.

I still believe these statements, and they remain the main reasons why I continue to reach out to you, dear reader, in whatever capacity I can.

I'm praying for you. I'm cheering you on. You can do it. I know you can.

Your friend,

Bernadine

One more thing...

*I know I said you were done, but I just wanted to give you one last opportunity to doodle, **add some color, and write one more note, maybe two... ready? Just turn the page...***

Shh... Secret Fact
about your quest companion

I'll always pray for you dear reader. I'm so honored you chose my book.

Final assignment

Write a letter to yourself. Talk about your future goals. Be sure to tell your future self how you don't plan to let your mistakes define you and stop you from achieving success. Make it as detailed as you want. It's for your eyes only, unless you decide to share.

God's Dream Girl is...

Forgiven
She has confessed her sins and asked God's forgiveness.
1 John 1:9

Forgiving
She forgives as God has forgiven her.
Colossians 3:13

Loving
She loves because, she knows God, and God is love.
1 John 4:8

Obedient
She obeys God because she loves Him.
John 14:15

Determined
She puts her best effort into everything she does.
Ecclesiastes 9:10

Beautiful
She is fearfully and wonderfully made by God.
Psalm 139:14

I am God's Dream Girl!

Use the above list as an example and come up with your own list of qualities for God's dream girl. Write the list on next page.

God's Dream Girl is..

ACKNOWLEDGMENTS

If you fail to act on them, dreams will always remain just dreams!

I am so grateful to everyone who assisted me in following my dream of publishing this Bible Study for Young Ladies. It was a long journey to get to this moment and I am so thankful for your encouragement and assistance along the way.

My Heavenly Father, who gives me words and the desire to write them.

My husband, *Mark*, who encourages me daily.

My mom, *Pastor Monvella McIntosh*, who awaits me in heaven. *You always believed in me.*

My sisters, *Melonie, Stephanie* and my adopted sister *Bertha*, who always cheer me on.

My *nieces* and *cousins* who were some of my go to sources on, "*how a teen girl thinks*".

My Girl Talk group (their moms) and all the young ladies, (especially in my East Grand Bahama Community) who allowed me the privilege of being a part of their lives over the years.

To everyone who read multiple drafts of my book, *Mandie, Dishawne, Racquel, Melonie, Stephanie, Lynnette, Cleora, Chevette* and my most helpful and invaluable guide throughout this publishing process, *Alisa Wagner*, I appreciate the gift of your time, feedback and suggestions.

To my blogging friends who have read my posts, encouraged me in my writing journey over the years, and allowed me to share your blogging platform, especially, *Iris Nelson, Lisa Shaw* and *Alisa Wagner*. I am blessed by your kindness.

Beverly Mather, Madeline Stubbs & *Rachel's Daughters Mentoring Group* – You were the platform for the speech that evolved into this book. Thank you for the opportunity to share with you.

To my family and friends, thank you for always encouraging me with my writing. I couldn't have done it without you.

About the Author

Bernadine Zimmerman believes that young ladies need consistent, positive female mentors in their lives and has had the privilege to fill that role for many young ladies. Her sisters were her role models growing up and they inspired in her the desire to be the same for other young ladies.

Highlighting the positive in the lives of young ladies is important to Bernadine. To encourage and motivate teens she founded and published a quarterly magazine, *Keeping it Real Girl Talk*, an inspirational magazine specifically for teen girls. She did this between 2000-2010. Each issue of the magazine featured a young lady who was a positive role model in her school and community.

Bernadine has a Bachelor's Degree in primary Education and taught primary school for sixteen years. She also taught Sunday School for over ten years and often facilitated girls only Sunday School classes where they talked about issues relating to young ladies. Bernadine has also been a speaker at Girl's Clubs and events and hosted Girl Talk weekends at her home with 4-6 girls at a time. Her message whether written or spoken is always meant to encourage and inspire young women to trust God with their lives and follow their dreams.

This small-town island girl from the beautiful island of Grand Bahama left her island paradise over two years ago, to marry the love of her life, Mark. She now calls the huge state of Texas home. A quietly opinionated bookworm, Bernadine loves family, friends, coffee, laughter, Jesus, and red lipstick, just not necessarily in that order.

To find out more about Bernadine, or to contact her please visit her personal blog: trustinghimwithtoday.blogspot.com.

www.ingramcontent.com/pod-product-compliance
Lightning Source LLC
LaVergne TN
LVHW051500070426
835507LV00022B/2855